Annie Bananie
My Forever Home

For Richard and Mary Barden, dear
long-time friends of the Gaines family.
How my parents loved you!
Blessings Always,
Anne Farley Gaines, the illustrator
of "Annie Bananie"
2010 South Haven

Published in the United States 2009 by
Monica Joyce
Find out more about Annie Bananie or to contact the author visit Annie's website at
www.anniebananiewebsite.com

Copyright © 2009 by Monica Joyce

Annie Bananie
Written by Monica Joyce
Book Design by Design One Three, Inc.
Copyright © 2009, Illustrations by Anne Farley Gaines

All rights reserved. No part of this publication may be reproduced or transmitted in any form or by any means, electronic or mechanical, including photocopy, recording, or any information storage or retrieval system now known or to be invented without permission in writing from the publisher.

Annie Bananie
My Forever Home

Written by Monica Joyce

Special thanks to my sister Judy, librarian at Boone Elementary School in Chicago and her students for loving Annie and encouraging me to publish her story.

Annie Bananie
My Forever Home

This book is dedicated to all animals waiting

and hoping for a "forever" home.

From the sale of each book, a donation will be made to a local

Animal Humane Organization.

My name is Annie Bananie.

I am a small white poodle with lots of curly hair and big brown eyes. I am now 16 years old, but I hardly look it. I've had different names and different homes and with each came a new adventure, while I searched for my "forever home."

Annie Bananie
My Forever Home

1

As a puppy I came to live with an elderly man named Henry. We lived in a cozy house with a small back yard. Henry named me Fifi because Fifi is a French name, and since I'm a French poodle that name suited me just fine.

Henry and I were always together. We were best friends. Henry's eyesight was not very good so he didn't drive much. I really didn't like car rides anyway because it usually meant I had to go to the veterinarian and get shots or go to the groomer. I didn't like getting baths, but I liked the pink ribbons that were put in my hair and how good I smelled when the groomer was finished. Sometimes I would get a spray of perfume. Henry would tell me how good I was and how pretty I looked. He said I was the most beautiful dog in the world.

Henry and I went almost everywhere together. But when I couldn't go along, I would curl up in Henry's big brown furry slippers. Henry's slippers were soft and warm. Here I would always wait for him to return.

Henry had a son named Jack who came to visit him occasionally. Jack didn't like dogs so he would never pet me, talk to me, or give me treats. When I was seven years old, Henry became sick and so Jack frequently took Henry to the doctor. Sometimes, when I heard them talking I would hear my name and Henry seemed upset.

One day Jack took Henry to the hospital. He took Henry's slippers with, so I had nowhere warm and soft to wait for him. I was so lonely I curled up in Henry's favorite chair and waited. I worried and worried since Henry had never left with his slippers before.

Later that night, Jack came and drove me to a place I had never been. Jack didn't speak to me, and I knew something bad was happening. When I got to this new place I could hear lots of dogs barking. I was so frightened I was shaking.

Jack handed me to a man who carried me off and put me in a big room in a small cage with all the other dogs. There were big dogs and medium size dogs and small dogs like me. But none of them seemed very happy to be there.

Most dogs only stayed a week or two. They told me their owners went on vacation. They didn't like being there, but they knew it wouldn't be for long. I made friends with some of them, but just as I got to know them, their owners came and took them home. I waited and waited. I wished I had Henry's soft furry slippers to curl up in while I waited. But Henry never came home.

One day, 6 months later, Jack called the kennel. Jack didn't want me and he wasn't going to try find me a home. He knew I was already seven years old, and since most people wanted puppies or younger dogs, he didn't even try. But Katy, a worker at the kennel, wanted me to have a home. She was very kind to me. Every day she took me for a walk and she gave me a special treat.

Sometimes she would give me a bath. And even though there were no ribbons for my hair or perfume, she grew to love me. She remembered that her Grandma Myrtle loved dogs and thought Grandma Myrtle could use a new friend.

Annie Bananie

My Forever Home

2

At first Grandma Myrtle wasn't sure if she wanted another dog, but Katy kept asking her over and over again. Finally Grandma Myrtle said I could come over for a visit. I was so excited to leave this place that I didn't even mind the car ride. I knew I was on a brand new adventure and I was going to like this one.

Katy told me lots of nice things about Grandma Myrtle. Still I was very nervous. I wanted her to like me. I hadn't been groomed in a long time. Katy brushed my hair, and tried her best to make me look pretty. Just like Henry, she told me I was beautiful and she put pink ribbons in my hair! That gave me some hope. She told me I was special and that Grandma Myrtle was going to like me very much. I had a hard time sitting still in Katy's car. Maybe just maybe, this would be my forever home.

Grandma Myrtle lived in a big red house with a big front porch. When we arrived, Grandma Myrtle and her daughter Candy were sitting on the front porch waiting.

Grandma Myrtle picked me right up and gave me a big hug. She had pretty white hair and wore an apron that held a special treat for me in the pocket.
Grandma Myrtle indeed decided to keep me.

I was so happy and relieved and felt so much at home that I curled up in her fluffy white slippers and fell sound asleep.

With my new home came a new name. Grandma Myrtle soon decided to name me Annie after the book Little Orphan Annie. I was to spend the next seven years living with her and Candy in their big house with their big front porch. Candy was very kind and took good care of us. She would take me to the groomer where I would get ribbons in my hair and a spray of perfume. We were just like a family. I loved Grandma Myrtle and my new home and even my new name.

As years passed, Grandma Myrtle walked slower and slower. Sometimes she would have to use a cane so she wouldn't fall. We couldn't take many walks anymore, or visit the neighbors. But we would go into the yard whenever the weather was good. When it was too cold to go out, Grandma Myrtle would sit in her favorite chair by the window and read. I would watch for the mailman, letting out my most ferocious bark, warning Grandma Myrtle of his arrival. I would then curl up next to her and fall fast asleep.

Grandma Myrtle and I were growing old together. I began to lose my eyesight. I knew the rooms in the big house very well, so even though I became blind I could make my way around. I also lost most of my teeth because of old age. But Grandma Myrtle and Candy made sure I had special soft food that I could chew.

Suddenly Grandma Myrtle began to feel ill, and Candy had to take her to the doctor often. I would wait in Grandma Myrtle's fluffy white slippers. I worried and worried about her. Months later Grandma Myrtle grew worse and had to spend most of her days in bed. I stayed close by and would lie next to her and keep her company.

One day began like all the others, but I knew something was wrong with Grandma Myrtle. I couldn't help worrying. I stayed close to her, and wouldn't leave her side. I didn't want to eat or go into the yard.

Later that night Grandma Myrtle died. Candy and I cried together. Now it was just me and Candy in Grandma Myrtle's big house. Candy would go to work every day, and I would wait for her to return while sleeping in Grandma Myrtle's slippers.

Candy was soon to be married, and the house had to be sold. Candy couldn't take me with her. I feared I would have to go back to the kennel or worse. Candy asked many friends if anyone wanted me but no one did.

Some people made fun of the way I looked. They thought I was ugly. I was blind and needed special food and medicine. I wasn't very pretty any more. But Candy wouldn't give up. She said she would find me a home. I was hopeful that maybe someone would want me and love me just like Henry and Grandma Myrtle. In fact, something told me I was headed for a new adventure.

Finally, a lady named Monica who loved animals said she would take me. She already had two dogs, named Motts and Sunshine. I wondered, would they like me since I was old and blind and not pretty anymore?

Soon it was time to go to my new home. Candy packed up my medication and the little bed Grandma Myrtle gave me and off we went.

Annie Bananie
My Forever Home

3

When we arrived at my new home everyone was waiting for me. Sunshine and Motts rushed to greet me. Sunshine was a kind and gentle golden retriever. She too was getting old and had gray whiskers to prove it. Motts, a goldendoodle, was only a year old. He was a very big shaggy dog, who acted as silly as he looked. He was always happy. Both welcomed me to their home. Candy brought special treats and toys for Sunshine and Motts. Motts was so happy he ran all over the house with his new toys, hoping I would play with him.

My first day at my new house I was nervous and scared. I kept bumping into things. I was shaking a lot and Monica had to sit and hold me. Though Candy had brought my bed, my first night I found Monica's fluffy warm slippers and fell fast asleep in them.

This house was very busy and noisy and not like the other houses I lived in. Soon I was able to find my way around the house and the yard and not bump into things. I even got used to silly Motts.

Monica's son Ian was very playful. Sometimes he carried me around dancing and spinning until we were dizzy. We had lots of fun. When we weren't busy playing we would sit together and watch television. I was having so much fun with this big, new family that I soon began to feel younger than my fourteen years.

My new block had many nice neighbors with lots of children. I was afraid they might make fun of me, but soon they came to know me and ask if they could take me for a walk or carry me up and down the block. They made sure I didn't bump into things like trees and bushes that sometimes got in my way. Sometimes one of the children would tuck me under their arm and take me rollerblading. We went so fast that I felt like I was flying. I was glad to have so many new friends and neighbors.

And, since Monica liked to sing and rhyme things,
she named me Miss Annie Bananie.
That's what all my friends call me now.

Every day we would go to the doggie park together, where there were all kinds of dogs who came with their owners to run and play. Many of them came from shelters hoping too for a forever home. Some were found on the street, dirty and hungry. One was even a Katrina dog, rescued from the flood waters of New Orleans. They were excited to meet any newcomer, and ran up and sniffed and barked.

At first, I was frightened, but I soon got used to all the noise. Motts always kept a watchful eye on me. He seemed to know I couldn't see, and so became my eyes when we were at the park.

One hot summer day as we sat by Monica's friend, George's swimming pool, I heard the buzz of what sounded like a big yellow bumblebee. It landed on the tip of my nose over and over. I was getting madder and madder, and so I finally decided to take things into my own hands and chased it. But I got too close to the edge of pool and suddenly slipped and fell in.

I found myself under water tumbling toward the bottom of the pool. I frantically doggie paddled trying to make my way to the top, but I kept falling. I was almost out of breath when George spotted me and sprung to his feet, and with the net on the long pole quickly scooped me up out of the water and saved me. I was so scared I was shaking. I was dripping wet, so Monica wrapped me in a towel and held me tight. When I finally dried off she fixed the ribbons in my hair and I looked just fine again. From that day on I stayed far away from the pool, and Monica kept a watchful eye on me.

No sooner did I think that all my adventures were over when Monica packed a bunch of bags and my bed and put everyone in the car. We were all going up to the summer home in Wisconsin.

Lake Delavan was very different from my home. The sounds and smells of ducks and rabbits were everywhere. In the early morning, I awakened to flocks of geese chattering away. But the hum from the motor of the fishing boats as they chugged down the channel lulled me back to sleep.

One day, when Monica was unloading the car, curiosity got the best of me, and I went exploring on my own. I took off down the road, over the bridge and around the channel. Soon, Monica realized I had disappeared. She ran up and down and all around trying to find me.

Finally one of the neighbors said she saw a little white poodle riding in a golf cart, over the bridge, down the channel to someone else's house. This family had a dog named Muffy that looked just like me. They thought I was Muffy and took me home. The best part was I got to have a ride on the golf cart up and down the channel. Soon Monica came to retrieve me, and everyone had a good laugh.

My most recent adventure was very scary for everyone. One October day Monica was raking leaves in the back yard, and I was sitting near by. Monica opened the gate for just a second, and I decided to go exploring. I walked down the alley, hoping to find some new smells, but I soon became confused. The more I walked the more confused I became.

Monica looked all over. She put up posters, called the police, animal shelters and local veterinarians. No one had seen me. She rode her bike up and down the streets. Neighbors helped. Signs were everywhere that said Annie Bananie was missing. Everyone knew I wouldn't be able to stay outside long. Even strangers asked about me, and promised to keep a look out for me.

But I had walked far from home. Somehow I had made it across several busy streets. Cars were honking their horns. They didn't know I was old and blind and couldn't go very fast. I was getting tired and hungry, and more and more lost. The wind was beginning to blow and I could hear the branches swaying. The crackle of thunder warned me a storm was coming.

I walked as quickly as I could, but found myself bumping into rocks and boulders. I was surrounded by grass and weeds much bigger than me. As I stumbled along, I could hear the trains' whistles blowing as they flew by heading into the train station just ahead. I was helplessly lost and frightened.

Just as I was beginning to give up hope, I heard footsteps and someone shouting to me. A kind lady saw me walking along the railroad tracks. Knowing the dangers that awaited me she quickly scooped me up and we hurried away.

I knew I was very lucky. And since I was so tired she carried me to her home.
She fed me and made me a bed out of blankets, and promised we'd look for my home.

The next two days my new friend walked me around the neighborhood looking for Monica. But we couldn't find my home.

Finally after three days my new friend called the animal shelter and they called Monica. Everyone there had remembered the missing blind poodle. My new friend lived close to George, and so once again he sprung up and ran right over to get me. Everyone in the neighborhood was happy I was back home.

All the children on the block came to welcome me back. I was so happy to be home and tired from my adventure that I crawled into Monica's fluffy slippers and fell sound asleep.

I've decided, at least for now, to avoid adventures and stay close to home. After all, this is my forever home.

Author's Note
the Plight of the Older Dog

"Nobody ever wants them, and they become profoundly depressed as they languish in cages at shelters. They've had good homes, but their luck ran out. Often their owner died, moved away, or was put in a nursing facility." These were the words of my friend Elaine, that echoed in my head when asked if I would give Annie a home.

Why anyone would want a 14-year-old poodle, especially one who is blind and requires special medicine and food, I thought. Certainly not me, who already had two dogs and a horse to tend.

But I remembered the story Elaine told me months before. Elaine was a Humane Society Veterinarian who knew all too well the plight of the older dog. She knew who usually gets adopted and who doesn't. She watched families and individuals walk by the cages of the older dogs searching for a puppy or a young dog.

"People want puppies and young dogs. They forget the work involved in house-breaking and training or how many walks it takes to wear them out. The older dogs just want a home and someone to love them. They don't ask for much; a warm place to live, food and a little love. They make wonderful pets and are so grateful to have a home again," she told me.

"No one wants Annie; too old, blind, she'll never survive another change. Even her veterinarian recommends putting her down. Please won't you give her a chance?" These were the words of a friend as she begged me to take Annie.

Did Annie deserve another chance? Even at the age of 14? Will she ever fit into my busy lifestyle, I wondered. As you'll see in the story of Annie's last two years not only did she survive the change but enjoyed life to the fullest.

- Monica Joyce -

About the Author

Monica Joyce is a nutritionist and diabetes educator living and working in Chicago, Illinois. Monica authored **Pluck, Spunk and Grit**, an anthology of stories and poems from children with Type 1 diabetes.

She is the founder of The Slam Dunk for Diabetes Basketball Camp, an organization sponsored by the Chicago Bulls professional basketball team. This scholarship camp is free to all children with diabetes, ages 5 to 18 years.

Annie Bananie was written as a testament of the love, joy and special relationship of adopting and owning an older dog. By sharing her experience with Annie Bananie, Monica hopes to inspire others to consider adopting an older dog. "Please won't you give them a **chance.**"

About the Illustrator

Anne Farley Gaines is an artist specializing in both traditional and innovative portraits, landscapes, and florals. Anne lives in Chicago, Illinois and is an adjunct instructor of design at the International Academy of Design and Technology in Chicago.

Annie Bananie
My Forever Home

Made in the USA
Charleston, SC
31 March 2010